Tapp

MW01502906

The Beginner's Guide To Clearing Energy Blocks and Manifesting More Money Using Emotional Freedom Technique

LISA TOWNSEND

Table of Contents

Introduction

Welcome to my beginner's guide to the Emotional Freedom Technique (EFT or "tapping") for wealth and abundance! In this book, we'll take an in-depth look at what tapping is, why it works, and how to use it effectively to increase your ability to *attract*, *receive*, and *have* all the wealth and abundance you want and deserve.

We'll begin with an overview of the origins and development of EFT, and a discussion about why it works. Then we'll cover what's known as the "Basic Recipe," essentially the basic structure of *how* to tap, in depth. This is a useful exercise even if you already have some familiarity with the technique, as you'll gain a deeper understanding of the how's and whys. We'll also cover some helpful tips for using EFT effectively.

One thing that has been clearly established from the experience of hundreds of EFT practitioners over the years is that the results you achieve depend a great deal on the correct implementation of the technique. For this reason, I've included several complete tapping "scripts" and diagrams to help you tap correctly. I want to be sure that you have all the information you need to start off on the right foot and avoid common pitfalls that may slow your progress.

Of course, in this book our focus is on how to use tapping to access greater wealth and abundance, so most of the content deals with that subject specifically. I've devoted a section each to the subjects of **attracting, receiving, and having money**, because these three aspects are all equally important in the creation an abundant life.

While this book provides a rich introduction to everything you need to know to start tapping on your own, **I want to emphasize that the best results may be obtained by**

working with a trained EFT facilitator. There are many subtle ways in which progress can be blocked, but they can all be addressed by a skilled facilitator who has learned how to apply advanced approaches to the technique. Also, the technique was originally designed to address the emotional underpinnings of physical problems, so it often evokes strong emotional reactions. If you feel that the subject of money may carry an especially strong emotional charge for you, then I strongly advise you to seek the support of a trained facilitator before you begin to explore tapping on your own.

EFT, or tapping, has helped countless people help themselves in every area of life. I've put this book together in the hope that it will help you physically, emotionally, and spiritually to become a powerful magnet for the money you need to live a life you love.

Lisa Townsend

What Is the Emotional Freedom Technique?

The Emotional Freedom Technique (EFT) is a method of psychological acupressure that anyone can use to perform simple and effective self-healing in minutes. It was created in the 1990s by Gary Craig, an acupuncturist who realized that too often, even holistic medicine fails to address the emotional roots of disease. He developed EFT as a form of energy medicine that involves tapping on acupressure points with the fingers (in place of acupuncture needles) to release the energy blockages responsible for mental, emotional, and physical dis-ease. This is why EFT is sometimes referred to as "tapping." Mr. Craig spent several years perfecting the technique before publishing *The EFT Manual* in 1996. Since then, the popularity of EFT has exploded, with many people creating their own innovations based on their experiences with the method.

One of the wonderful things about EFT is its simplicity, yet many people have trouble believing it's so simple, and thus make it more complicated than it really is. In this section, we'll cover everything you'll need to know about what EFT is, how it works, and how to begin "tapping" successfully now. You may wish to go over this section a couple of times so you can be sure you understand the basics, before moving on to the sections specific to wealth and abundance.

The Theory Behind EFT – Why it Works

EFT is based on traditional Chinese medicine's understanding of the energetic aspects of the body and mind. In this healing system, energy channels called meridians are believed to exert a powerful influence on the mind-body system. In traditional acupuncture, tiny needles are inserted into areas of the body where these meridians are believed to exist, with the goal of unblocking the flow of life-force energy, or *qi*, to activate the body's self-healing mechanism. In sharp contrast to *Western* medicine, *Chinese* medicine is all about prevention and addressing problems at their root, rather than focusing on symptoms alone. In ancient China, people made regular preventative visits to their doctors to maintain their health, and paid them only as long as they remained well. When someone got sick, the doctor was held responsible, and received no further payment until they successfully restored the person's health. Pretty much the polar opposite of the system we have in the Western world today!

Traditional Chinese Medicine, and acupuncture in particular, have been in continuous use for thousands of years. It is now widely practiced around the world, because millions of people successfully found relief from a wide variety of illnesses with it, particularly those with conditions like autoimmune disorders that respond poorly to Western medicine. More than anything, the "eastern" approach appeals to people who desire a more holistic style of healthcare. People who receive acupuncture treatments are often surprised to find that they also feel better emotionally, but it makes sense when you consider that the body and mind are *one system*. This is where the power of EFT comes from.

Gary Craig and his mentor, Dr. Roger Callahan, built their work around the idea that blockages in the meridians might play a major role not only in physical ailments, but emotional ones as well. They then took this insight a step further, hypothesizing that energy meridians might provide *a direct way to fully and permanently release the negative mental-emotional patterns responsible for the creation of our reality through the Law of Attraction.* To put it another way, *EFT provides a simple, practical, and highly-effective way to actually change your point of attraction at the level of energy.* At the heart of theory about why EFT works is what its founder calls The Discovery Statement, which is simply this:

The cause of all negative emotions is simply a disruption in the body's energy system.

By the mid-1990s, many people were already aware of the principles behind the Law of Attraction, but were becoming frustrated by assurances that simply "changing their thinking" would be enough, when for so many it didn't seem to work that way. When those people discovered EFT, they realized they had found the missing link that could help them change not only their conscious mental and emotional states, but also the energy mechanisms that anchored the problematic states subconsciously. Over years of experimentation, it was found that EFT could help successfully address issues ranging from phobias and addictions to physical pains.

The idea that dis-ease at every level results from blockages in the meridians, and that these can be released by tapping on various "end points" of meridians located in the upper body, while focusing on the problem and its solution, is basically the core of how EFT works. In the next section, we'll go over the basic structure of how tapping is physically done and how a session is constructed, known as "The Basic Recipe", which is the scaffolding around which all variations of EFT are built. I'll explain in detail why each step is crucial to the effectiveness of the technique, and answer common questions that beginners often have at this stage.

The "Basic Recipe"

The power of EFT lies in the unique combination of its two core elements: activating acupressure points through tapping, and verbally stating a problem with an affirmation that counteracts the problem. In EFT, the Basic Recipe refers to the four core elements of the verbal statements that accompany a round of tapping. In this section, I will describe proper tapping technique and the precise locations to tap on, as well as how to create the most effective verbal "scripts" for tapping. We will look at each element in isolation, then bring them all together to form a complete tapping sequence. **I strongly encourage you to review this section several times before you begin practicing EFT for the first time.** It'll be well worth it.

Tapping: Locations and Technique

In this section, I'll cover what you need to know to do the actual tapping portion of EFT effectively. While I'll provide you with clear and complete instruction here, there are countless video tutorials online, and it can be invaluable to watch someone else go through the sequence a few times if you are a visual learner. For this reason, I suggest that you take a few minutes to search online for a video that resonates with you, and use it to complement what you learn here. You can even follow along with the practitioner, until the sequence becomes embedded in your muscle memory. While the tapping itself is important, it is most effective when you don't need to think about it too much, and can focus instead on the process of release. For this reason, it's good to practice the tapping alone a few times without a verbal script, before you try the complete EFT technique for the first time.

As I mentioned before, the points that we tap on in EFT are the "end points" of major meridians. However, there are also smaller end points at the tip of each finger, which gives your tapping an extra boost. While the original method developed by Gary Craig used only the index and middle fingers of one hand while tapping, people have found that using more fingers and/or both hands works equally well or better. Dr. Joseph Mercola, who writes extensively of his own experiences with EFT on his website, believes that tapping with all four fingers and both hands increases the potency of the technique. He also recommends tapping with the two hands slightly out of sync. In any case, you want to be sure to tap the points with your fingertips, not the pads of your fingers, because this won't activate the fingertip meridians. If you do tap with only one hand, there is no reason you can't switch hands/sides any time you wish to. You should tap firmly, but never so hard that it hurts.

Now that you know how to tap, it's time to learn where to tap. You may wish to bookmark the following diagram, Figure 1, and the explanation that follows. Please note that the points to tap on are indicated by the black dots in the diagram.

Each point is listed below with its standard abbreviation, in the top-to-bottom order that is the conventional tapping sequence:

- Karate Chop (KC)
- Top of Head (TH)
- Eyebrow (EB)
- Side of Eye (SE)
- Under Eye (UE)
- Under Nose (UN)
- Chin (Ch)
- Collarbone (CB)
- Under Arm (UA)
- Wrist (WR)

Figure 1

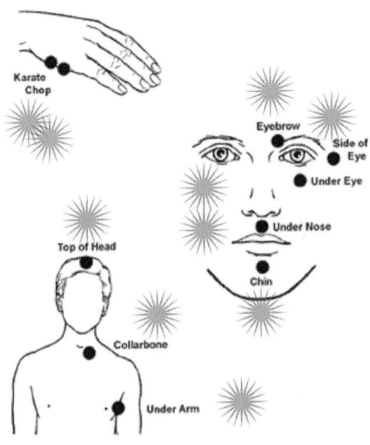

It doesn't actually matter in which order you tap, as long as you cover them all, but the convention of starting at the top of the head and working down helps people remember each point.

EFT is predicated on what's called "the 100% overhaul concept." There's no easy way to tell which meridian is responsible for a given problem so by tapping on all the points, doing a "total energetic overhaul," you improve the chances that you're going to clear the one that's causing the issue in question. It's like a starting a cake recipe over when you realize the batter is too runny; you may not remember which ingredient you messed up the first time, but to get it right you need to redo, or reset in the case of meridians, the whole thing. Tapping on an un-blocked meridian won't hurt it, while covering them all in the best way to ensure you get the problem one or ones.

Ingredients for the Basic Recipe

EFT practitioners use the metaphor of a recipe for the technique because it highlights the importance of not only using the right ingredients, but of doing things in the right sequence. Both are important for the technique to be effective.

Below are the steps to include in the Basic Recipe:

1. Choose a "Problem" to work on.
2. Rate the intensity of distress caused by the problem between one and 10.
3. Create the "Setup" statement.
4. Tap the sequence of points while repeating the "Reminder Phrase."
5. Rate the intensity again, and do additional rounds if necessary.

In the following section, we'll take a closer look at each step in isolation. Then, we'll look at some sample "tapping scripts" so that you can learn how to put them all together into a complete round of tapping.

Step 1: Choose a Problem

The first step is to choose the specific emotion, traumatic event, or physical issue that you will focus on for this round of tapping. Sometimes beginners over-think this step because they believe that they must choose exactly the right thing to tap on, or they will not experience results. However, you can almost always make progress just by tapping on whatever is on your mind at the moment. Gary Craig often exhorts his students to "try it on everything," knowing that many of our subconscious issues are interconnected, and we don't need to understand exactly how in order for EFT to work. His experience, and that of many others, with the technique has been that if we just tap on whatever's bothering us right now, that is usually effective. The important thing is to consistently practice EFT as a tool for daily self-healing.

There are a couple of finer points to this that we will go over in later sections, but for now, we will simply look at some general examples that might come up specifically around issues of wealth and abundance:

1. Fear that I won't have enough money for retirement
2. Fear that I won't have enough money to pay the bills next month
3. Fear that if I accumulate wealth, I will only lose it again
4. Belief that having money means I'm not spiritual
5. Belief that having money means I'm an "evil rich person"
6. Fear that having money will make my life too complicated
7. Fear that having money will change my relationships
8. Belief that it's not possible to do what I love and make a living at it
9. The time in 3rd grade when those big kids beat me up and stole my lunch money

10. The time in middle school when I went out with my friends only to realize my money had fallen out of my pocket and I couldn't pay for my meal after I had already eaten it

I want to draw your attention to #9 and 10, because it differs from all the other statements in an important way. Rather than focusing on a general emotion, these statements refer to a *specific traumatic memories* that carry a negative emotion. In general terms, you could state the problems as "fear that having money is dangerous" Or "I can't hold on to money." However, what has emerged in the experience of hundreds of EFT practitioners is that the most effective approach is often to list all the events that trigger a certain negative emotion in descending order of intensity, then tap your way through the list from top to bottom. In *The EFT Manual*, Gary Craig calls this *The Personal Peace Procedure*, and we'll devote more space to it later in the book.

You can use the general examples above to prompt you to remember emotionally-charged events from your life that may be affecting your ability to attract wealth. If you can't remember any such events, then using the statements "as-is" may provide some relief as well.. The benefits of the specific-event approach are obvious in situations like childhood abuse and war trauma, where there are clear memories of a series of distinct traumatic events. However, subtler issues like the ability to attract, receive, and have wealth may be harder to pin down in this way, and can therefore be addressed in more general terms at first.

Step 2: Rate the Intensity

This step is performed at the beginning and end of every tapping session, to give you a way to track your progress. It simply involves rating your current state of emotional distress from zero to 10,where zero is a complete lack of distress, and 10 is the most intense emotional pain imaginable. While in many cases, one round of tapping is enough to bring your level of distress down to zero, this is not always the case, and rating the intensity of your feelings before and after each round of tapping lets you know whether you're "done" or not. When one round is not enough, it usually means that there are one or more "aspects" to the problem that remain to be addressed. We'll go over how to identify and release the additional aspects later on.

For now, simply know that you will be starting and ending each round of tapping with this self-assessment of your current level of distress on a scale of zero to 10. If you find that a particular issue actually ranks quite low on the scale (between zero and two, let's say) when you think of it, you may wish to dig deeper until you find an emotion, event, or memory that is more emotionally charged. This is the principle behind the Personal Peace Procedure that I mentioned earlier. Practitioners of EFT have found that, if you rank issues in order of emotional intensity and work your way down, clearing the issues with the most charge also releases energy from issues further down the list.

Please note that is important to rate the intensity of your emotions *right now* as you begin or end your tapping session, *not as you expect them to be at a future event*. That is, if you are due for your annual review at work and are anxious at the thought of negotiating a raise with your boss, you need to tap on the anxiety you feel *now* when you think of that event, not what you *expect to feel* when you sit down at that meeting. The reason for this has to do with the fact that the subconscious mind is very literal, and can't process emotions that haven't yet arisen in present time. This is where you need to relax a bit and trust the process. **When you practice EFT consistently, you will train your subconscious to clear issues a piece at a time, at the pace that's right for you**. There's no need to overwhelm yourself by trying to fix problems you don't have yet. Simply work on whatever's up for you right now, and let go of the rest. One of the beautiful things about EFT is that it gives us a way to consciously participate in our own healing without needing to understand the mystery behind the process.

Step 3: Create the "Setup"

In EFT, the Setup refers to the spoken phrase that states both the problem you will address, and an affirmation that creates space for its release. **I want to emphasize the importance of keeping this *as simple as possible*.** If you search online, you will find many video tutorials in which experienced EFT practitioners go through tapping sequences, and most of them vary their setup phrasing quite a bit throughout a given round. While this is fine to do once you become more experienced, *I believe that even experienced practitioners lose some of the potency of the technique when they make the verbal statements too complicated.* This is because when you get too caught up in verbal gymnastics, you can't focus as fully on calling up the energetic blockages that you intend to clear. **What you say is much less important than your ability to hold your focus on the blockage as you tap to clear it.** If your intention is strong when you choose your initial wording, there's no need to trip yourself up by changing it midway through your tapping. Yet, because so many instructors in online tutorials do it this way, many beginners get stymied by wording, when the important thing is really to focus on the emotion and the tapping itself.

When you create the Setup for a tapping session, there are four important things to keep in mind:

1. Keep It Simple!
2. State the Problem as Specifically as Possible.
3. Choose a Self-Affirming Affirmation.
4. Choose a Reminder Phrase to Help You Focus on the Problem While Tapping.

I've already addressed #1 in the paragraph above.

With regard to #2, one of the most common mistakes made by people new to EFT is to state their problem in terms that are too general. Again, this is due to what the practice of EFT (and other similar techniques) has taught us about the literal nature of the subconscious mind.

When you state a problem, what is happening at an energetic level is that you are "calling up a file," like opening a file on your computer, that contains the blockage in your meridian system so that it can be cleared. Think of "calling up the file" as opening up a memory, or activating a feeling you have repeatedly around a topic.

Continuing with our computer metaphor, the feeling is really a marker telling you there is a big "program" running there. The problem is your subconscious doesn't know how to *clear* issues at the "file level" it just knows how to run the program, or experience that, which is *in* the file. So it's up to you to pay attention to the emotions that are showing you where the energetically problematic programs and files are.

As an example let's say we're dealing with chronic low self-worth. There are probably dozens of different "files" (memories, associations, and emotions) which the subconscious constantly runs (the program again) that create the overall effect of low self-worth. Using our computer metaphor, you can "crash" the program, or destroy the problem, by clearing and wiping out the problematic files, or memories, one at a time. So we clear one file at a time, such as "the time I got an A- on my report card and my father criticized me," or "I'm afraid that no matter what I do, it'll never be enough," until the program is missing so many files that it collapses and can no longer run, meaning your experience of the problem is a zero on our discomfort scale.

Clearing things this way may seem inefficient, but when we consider the "generalization effect" that I mentioned earlier, it is actually the most effective way to remove energetic blocks. This is another reason to simply tap on whatever specific emotion or event is coming up for you at a given moment (whether related to wealth and abundance or any other issue.)

Point #3 refers to the affirmation that you will use to activate healing of the problem in the Setup. With the expansion of EFT have come myriad variations in the types of affirmations that are used in the Setup, but I firmly believe in sticking to the kind of self-affirming statement italicized below, especially at first:

"Even though I (problem statement), *I deeply and profoundly love and accept myself."*

It doesn't matter whether you "believe" the affirmation or not, saying it is still powerful. The creators of EFT intuitively understood that the road to healing almost any problem begins with self-love and acceptance, and the experience of many practitioners has reinforced this idea. In the section of his website that he devotes to EFT, Dr. Joseph Mercola gives his perspective on the importance of self-affirmation:

When I first started doing the EFT work, I modified the affirmation and tried substituting phrases like "I choose to remain calm and relaxed," and a variety of other ones that I thought might be better. However, the more I studied this issue, the more I realized that self-love is at the core of most of our issues....You can use the EFT affirmations to help you address [what] seems to be the key to most people's health problems, which is loving yourself and a peaceful transformation of your self-criticism. Everyone has made negative choices in the past, we all have. The good news is that we all have a choice. You can always choose to let go of the old pattern...Letting go of your old negative pattern with love allows you to move into the new pattern with ease.

There is something about combining a statement of the problem at hand with a statement of complete acceptance of yourself as you are that carries a great deal of power. Elsewhere in his discussion of EFT, Dr. Mercola strongly encourages practicing your EFT affirmations (and the tapping itself when possible) in front of a mirror while staring into one's own eyes. Just to imagine doing this will intensify emotion for many people, and in EFT that's a good thing, because it means you're addressing the issue at a deeper level.

On the subject of emotion, there is a final detail of the basic recipe that I haven't addressed yet: **the Reminder Phrase**. The Reminder Phrase consists of the "problem" portion of your Setup, or a fraction of it if it is quite long. Its purpose is to help you keep the problem you are addressing "activated" in your field while you perform the tapping. You repeat it to yourself as you tap each point, to remind your subconscious of what it is releasing. So, for example:

Let's say your Setup is: *"Even though I have this fear that I won't have enough money to pay next month's rent, I deeply and profoundly love and accept myself."*

The reminder phrase is the underlined portion of the Setup, or a piece of it. You could condense it into *"not enough money for rent,"* or simply *"fear"* if you feel that will do the job. It is up to you to determine which reminder phrase will best "hold the charge" of the problem you intend to release.

As another example, let's say your Setup is: *"Even though I lost a house to foreclosure three years ago, I deeply and profoundly love and accept myself."*

This example illustrates how a reminder phrase looks when you're tapping on a specific event from the past that carries negative emotion.

A Note About Psychological Reversal

The Setup is designed to prime your energy system to receive maximum benefit from the tapping sequence. While experienced practitioners will sometimes skip it, it was put in place as part of EFT's "100% overhaul" approach in order to address a problem that Roger Callahan and Gary Craig call "psychological reversal," or PR for short. They claim that PR is to blame for the patterns of self-sabotage that so many of us struggle with.

In keeping with EFT's Discovery Statement, which asserts that *all negative emotion results from disruptions in the body's energy field*, psychological reversal is believed to result from a reversed polarity in an individual's electromagnetic field. Practitioners of EFT believe this is the primary reason why some people's problems don't respond to even the most proven therapeutic techniques. When PR is present, your subconscious automatically sabotages every effort you make to change. It is as if your energetic batteries are in backwards, and no amount of tapping (or other treatments) will work for you. While the concept of psychological reversal may be esoteric, it arose from Dr. Callahan's and Mr. Craig's direct experience working with patients. Since the correction for it is built into the Setup and takes only a few seconds, it's an easy base to cover.

On his website, Dr. Mercola notes that **you stand the best chance of removing all psychological reversal from your field when you speak the affirmation loudly and emphatically during the Setup.** It's been his observation that many of his patients need to nearly shout the affirmations in order to fully clear their channels for healing. The Setup is designed to address this, so the tapping can work.

If you'd like to understand it in greater depth, psychological reversal is covered quite extensively in Gary Craig's free *EFT Manual*. I mention it here only because, if you find that you are unable to achieve results despite tapping consistently over a period of a month or so, then a strong PR effect may be to blame. In that case, you would be best served by consulting a qualified EFT facilitator, who can work with you one on one to remedy it.

If you do become frustrated by a lack of progress, I deeply urge you not to give up on EFT until you have consulted with a professional EFT facilitator. You can find a database of clinical certified EFT practitioners at www.eftuniverse.com. On his website, Dr. Mercola notes that while EFT is one of the most effective self-healing techniques he knows of, in many cases patients experience much more dramatic results from working with a qualified facilitator, rather than on their own. He attributes this to the resonance provided by the facilitator's energy field, which combines with the patient's energy field to "amp up the power' available for the process. The most important thing to remember with EFT is that persistence pays. As with any program for self-improvement, your success depends on your consistent application of the technique.

Step 4: Tap the Sequence

In this section, I will lay out a complete tapping "script" that you can adapt to your own needs. Because the success of EFT seems to depend greatly on choosing a highly specific issue to tap on, I recommend that you use these scripts only for practice, substituting your own specific issues once you gain confidence. I have made an effort to include very common money-related issues in these scripts, so don't be surprised if using them does actually give you a greater feeling of freedom, even if they are not situation-specific to you. EFT is a powerful technique that works in mysterious ways, so optimism is a good policy!

Figure 2 contains a diagram of the points we will be tapping on the face, alongside a complete list of all the points in the sequence, which I will refer to by their abbreviations in the scripts. Refer to Figure 1 for a complete visual of all the points (except the inner wrists, which not all practitioners include). **Note: It's a good idea (but not strictly necessary) to remove eyeglasses, bracelets and / or watches before performing EFT to reduce potential interference.**

Notes on the Location of Certain Points

While most of the tapping points in EFT are straightforward to find, some are a little tricky, so I've included some tips on finding those below.

The Wrist Points (WR): The wrist points are just where you might fasten a watch on the inside of the wrists. While you could tap only one wrist with the fingers of the other hand, this sequence will ask you to tap the insides of both wrists together.

The Collarbone Points (CB): This point is at the junction where the sternum (breastbone), collarbone and the first rib meet. To locate it, first place your forefinger on the U-shaped notch at the top of the breastbone (about where a man would knot his tie). From the bottom of the U, move your forefinger down toward the navel 1 inch and then go to the left (or right) 1 inch. This point is referred to as Collar Bone even though it is not on the collarbone per se.

The Under-Arm Points (UA): On the side of the body, at a point even with the nipple for men, or in the middle of the bra strap for women. It is about four inches below the armpit.

Figure 2.

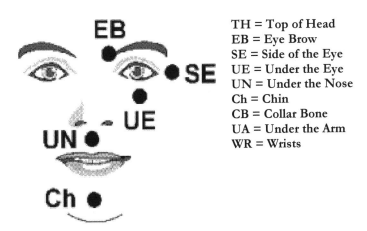

TH = Top of Head
EB = Eye Brow
SE = Side of the Eye
UE = Under the Eye
UN = Under the Nose
Ch = Chin
CB = Collar Bone
UA = Under the Arm
WR = Wrists

Step 5: Rate the Intensity Again, and Follow Up If Necessary

While EFT enthusiasts like to emphasize the fact that many issues can be resolved with only one round of tapping, this is not always the case, and you need to know what to do if you still feel some emotional charge after your first round. Again, the subconscious mind is very literal, so when you do follow-up rounds, you need to alert it to the fact that you are now clearing the *remaining* charge from the original issue. This is accomplished with the following simple adjustment to the Setup. To build on one of our earlier examples:

*"Even though I **still** have **some** of this fear that I won't have enough money to pay next month's rent, I deeply and profoundly accept myself."*

The underlined words are added to address the *remaining* fear, and the reminder phrase can be adjusted to *'remaining fear'* to maintain the focus on the aspects that still need to be cleared. While uncovering specific aspects may be helpful (a subject I will address later), in many cases simply directing the subconscious to clear whatever charge remains will be enough. Keep using the zero to ten scale to assess your progress, make consistent EFT practice a part of your day, and you'll be well on your way to success.

Let's Review The Basic Recipe

So, are you ready to put it all together into a full tapping sequence? Here's a recap of the basic recipe:

1. Choose a problem to work on.
2. Rate the intensity of distress caused by the problem.
3. Create the setup statement.
4. Tap the sequence of points while repeating the Reminder Phrase.
5. Rate the intensity again,.
6. Do additional rounds if necessary.

Next, I'll lead you through a complete tapping sequence that you can use right now to support you on your journey to wealth and abundance. Then, I'll wrap up this introductory section with tips and tricks to maximize the results of your tapping. After that, we'll dive deeper into how to use EFT specifically for money-related issues. Here's Figure 1 again, with a complete picture of the points you'll be tapping on:

Figure 1.

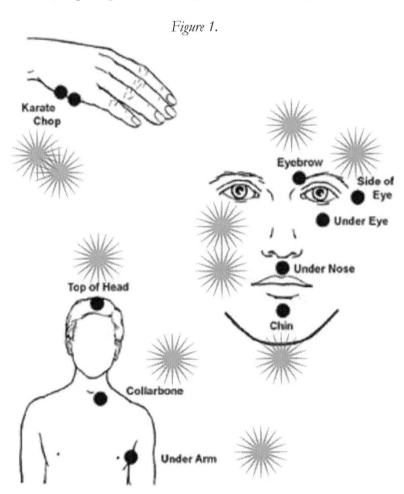

Have fun putting what you've learned into practice in the pages to come!

Get Ready to Tap

Step 1: Choose a Problem

For this sample script, we'll use an example that many people can relate to these days: the fear of not having enough money to retire comfortably.

Step 2: Rate the Intensity

At this point, we rate our *current* level of distress at the thought of not having enough money to retire comfortably. **Remember, you need to rate the level of distress you feel *right now*, not what you expect to feel at a future date.** Your subconscious mind lives in the now, and if you ask it to address a future problem, it can't release current ones.

Step 3: Create the Setup

In this script, we'll state the Setup as follows:

"Even though I have this fear that I won't have enough money to retire comfortably, I deeply love and accept myself."

For this sample tapping sequence, we'll use the following reminder phrase:

"not enough money to retire"

If this example happens to resonate for you (as it does for many of us), then make the most of this practice session with the following tips:

1. Remember that emotional intensity is **key** to tapping effectively. State your Setup and reminder phrase loudly and emphatically, to fully "call up the file," the memories and associations, of the negative emotion you intend to clear.
2. Don't tweak the wording; just stick with the example and focus on your tapping and emotional release. When you've practiced the tapping so much that you can do it without thinking, then you're ready to change the words.
3. Above all, **trust the process**!

Take your time with this sample script. May your path of healing into abundance with EFT begin now.

Sample Script for One Round of Tapping

Begin by noting your current level of distress on a scale of 0 – 10 (it's okay if it's a zero since this is a practice session; just focus on the tapping).

Next, move to the Setup. Repeat the following phrase three times while tapping the karate chop point (KC) of one hand with the index and middle fingers of the other. The more emphasis and emotion you can express here, the better!

KC - *"Even though I have this fear that I won't have enough money to retire comfortably, I deeply love and accept myself."*

KC - *"Even though I have this fear that I won't have enough money to retire comfortably, I deeply love and accept myself."*

KC - *"Even though I have this fear that I won't have enough money to retire comfortably, I deeply love and accept myself."*

Now, we'll tap through the full sequence of points (each listed by their abbreviations) while repeating the following reminder phrase. Tap each point firmly about seven times before moving on to the next one. Remember, the points are listed from highest to lowest on the body to facilitate your ability to remember them all.

Reminder Phrase: *"not enough money to retire"*

(TH) - *"not enough money to retire"*

(EB) - *"not enough money to retire"*

(SE) - *"not enough money to retire"*

(UE) - *"not enough money to retire"*

(UN) - *"not enough money to retire"*

(Ch) - *"not enough money to retire"*

(CB) - *"not enough money to retire"*

(UA) - *"not enough money to retire"*

(WR) - *"not enough money to retire"*

This completes one round. On the next page, we'll go through a 'follow-up' script that you would employ if you still felt some emotional charge around the issue after one round of tapping.

Sample Script for a Follow-Up Round

If you find that you still feel some charge after one round of tapping, you can make the following minor adjustments to your Setup and reminder phrase, then do another round of tapping to release any remaining emotional intensity.

Setup: *"Even though I **still** have **some** of this fear that I won't have enough money to retire comfortably, I deeply love and accept myself."*

Reminder Phrase: *"still some fear"*

Begin with the Setup:

KC - *"Even though I **still** have **some** of this fear that I won't have enough money to retire comfortably, I deeply love and accept myself."*

KC - *"Even though I **still** have **some** of this fear that I won't have enough money to retire comfortably, I deeply love and accept myself."*

KC - *"Even though I **still** have **some** of this fear that I won't have enough money to retire comfortably, I deeply love and accept myself."*

Then, proceed through the full tapping sequence:

TH: *"still some fear"*

EB: *"still some fear"*

SE: *"still some fear"*

UE: *"still some fear"*

UN: *"still some fear"*

Ch: *"still some fear"*

CB: *"still some fear"*

UA: *"still some fear"*

WR: *"still some fear"*

If you still feel some charge after this round, repeating the script a few more times is often enough to bring you to zero. In the next section, I'll discuss more tips for effective tapping, and what to do if you get stuck. These topics are more advanced, but I'll address them briefly to give you a glimpse of how a certified EFT facilitator may be able to help you overcome more complex issues.

With practice, you will be able to complete the entire tapping sequence in under a minute. As for how long to tap each point, a good guideline is to tap one point for a full breath (8 – 10 seconds for most people), or about seven times, before moving on to the next one.

More Tips for Tapping Effectively

Now that we've covered the Basic Recipe for EFT, I want to address some of the subtler factors that can influence your success with the technique. You may wish to further explore these either on your own, or with the support of a facilitator.

Aspects – Getting to the Root of Complex Problems

So far, we've explored EFT as a simple and effective tool for energy self-healing and emotional release. While this is the core of the technique however, it is not the whole story. Apart from emotional (and sometimes physical) healing, EFT is also invaluable as a tool for personal growth and awareness. In his extensive discussion of EFT on his website, Dr. Joseph Mercola describes the importance of paying attention to what he calls "cognitive shifts" when practicing EFT:

It is essential to pay attention to the cognitive shifts that can occur with even a single round of the tapping. A cognitive shift has occurred when you reframe the problem. Seeing the problem from a new angle, you will often express a sense of surprise and insight. These movements can offer valuable connections and associations and may open new pathways for healing. Following a cognitive shift, you often feel less guilt and self-blame, more hope, or a simple sense of relief in an area where there has never been relief before.

It is important to stop after tapping and see if you notice anything different, or if something new came up after you tapped. This is frequently the underlying issue that is the real root of your problem.

In the second paragraph, Dr. Mercola hints at the main strategy that tapping uses to address complex problems. When we find it difficult to state our problem in the kind of precise language that EFT requires, it is usually because we are focusing on a composite problem that contains numerous sub-problems, or "aspects." Because of the way the subconscious mind works, each of these aspects must be addressed individually in order for progress to be made. It's as if each aspect is a brick in the subconscious wall that keeps us from the life we want, and we must remove every brick in order to achieve our desired point of attraction.

The ability to discern aspects comes with practice, but even beginners can discover them by paying attention as they tap on the most specific statement of the problem that they can come up with. As you tap, notice any images, memories, or other thoughts that arise. These can point you to the next brick to release. Each time you finish a round, take a quiet moment to receive new insights and acknowledge any shifts you've made. The beauty of EFT is that it gives you a way to remove subconscious blocks one at a time, at the pace that's ideal for you. As you practice EFT consistently, you will find that your subconscious always brings up exactly the right aspect to clear at the right time. This is the result of your intention to let go of self-limitation and create your highest and best life, one step at a time.

Optimal Timing and Frequency of Tapping and Affirmations

In general, experienced EFT facilitators recommend tapping about 10 times per day for optimal results. This is not so much to ask when you consider that one round of tapping only takes about a minute. It's easier when you tie your tapping rounds to elements of your routine such as waking up and going to bed, eating, or going to the bathroom – taking a minute to tap at each of these points in your day will easily result in more than 10 rounds total. And as I've said before, consistency is probably the single most important factor in the success you experience with EFT, so it's worth a try.

If you can only tap once per day however, is there a particular time that is most ideal? There is, according to Dr. Mercola:

It is especially important to tap and say the affirmations before you go to sleep. This is probably the single most important time to do it. I can't encourage you enough to do the EFT affirmations every night. It is one of the most important principles I can give you. When you tap before you go to bed you will give your subconscious from 6-8 hours to work on your affirmations and help create them for you.

This has been his observation over many years of tapping on his own behalf, and many other practitioners agree. Dr. Mercola also notes that you can add power to any affirmation practice by tapping while you repeat the affirmations.

Activating the Power of Self- Love and Forgiveness

One thing that EFT shows us over and over again is that self-love is the key to healing, and that's why self-acceptance is built right into the Setup in the Basic Recipe.

While traditional Setup affirmations such as "I deeply love and accept myself" are well-suited to any tapping session, affirmations that target self-forgiveness may be appropriate when you realize you are beating yourself up. For many of us, a stream of self-berating thoughts runs through our subconscious like an underground river of pollution, which holds us back even if we are not aware of it most of the time. Practicing self-forgiveness regularly is a powerful way to not only feel more peaceful, but ***to expand your ability to receive***. I highlight this last part to illustrate how ***a lack of self-love can be one of the biggest things standing between you and the abundance you deserve***. For this reason, I recommend tapping for self-forgiveness at least once a day, either upon waking or before bed.

Here are some examples of self-forgiveness Setups from Dr. Mercola, who recommends doing this in front of a mirror:

You can look into your own eyes and say, "Even though I wasn't successful or I was angry or impatient or mean or cruel" or whatever problem you need to forgive yourself for, "I forgive myself, I was only doing the best I could," or, "I forgive you for holding onto those patterns for too long, I forgive you for not loving yourself."

Try it, you might be amazed at the results!

Making Your Affirmations Work for You

Many people who have practiced affirmations in other contexts are pleasantly surprised to find that repeating their affirmations while tapping seems to increase their potency. If using affirmations is new to you, consider yourself fortunate that you are beginning to implement them at the same time that you learn EFT. If you persist in repeating your affirmations while you tap at least once a day, over time chances are good that you will see results faster than you might without the tapping.

One very important tip about affirmations is that you *always want to phrase them in the present tense.* Again, the subconscious mind cannot grow the seed of a new thought in the future. It can only undertake that process in the present moment. So pay attention to how you word your affirmations, and make sure you don't say "I will feel" or "I am going to have," lest you slow down your transformation considerably.

As I mentioned before, affirmations that refer to self-love and acceptance seem to be the most effective, and their power will increase considerably if you say them in front of a mirror while looking into your own eyes. While this can be difficult, it is really worth doing if you want to achieve real change quickly. Remember that it doesn't matter whether you believe the affirmations you say or not, saying them will empower your mental/emotional body to achieve a point of attraction that is more in line with what you want to create. When it gets easier to look into your own eyes and say "I love you," then you know you are making progress!

Dr. Mercola speaks passionately about the importance of self-acceptance in his discussion of EFT:

Too many of us think we have to be bad or wrong before we can be changed, but we really don't have to do that. When you come from love and acceptance, the changes become much easier. You make a change because you want to improve the quality of your life, not because you are a bad person who wants to become better.

And when you know more, you will do things differently, so never, ever berate yourself for where you were.

Just tap in "I'm doing the best I can, I'm doing the best I can."

Remember, you need to constantly forgive yourself for not being perfect.

Later in this book, I'll devote a special section to common pitfalls that people new to tapping encounter, and address each individually. Now, however, it's finally time to look at how you can use EFT specifically to increase the flow of wealth and abundance in your life.

Why EFT for Wealth and Abundance?

By now, you're familiar with the Discovery Statement on which the theory of EFT is built: that *all negative emotions result from a disruption in the body's energy field.* If we accept this hypothesis (and the experience of thousands of EFT practitioners suggests that we can), and if we accept the Law of Attraction, we can see that *EFT is unique as a practical tool to help us consciously and permanently change our point of attraction.* The implications are revolutionary if we are serious about creating more wealth and abundance in our lives *at the level of energy.*

An interesting angle on this subject has been developed by Dr. Bruce Lipton, whose best-selling book <u>*The Biology of Belief*</u> popularized the idea that our thoughts control the expression of our genes (epigenetics). Because the vast majority of our thoughts are unconscious, Dr. Lipton has become increasingly interested in techniques that can effectively re-program the subconscious mind without depending solely on the conscious mind to bridge the gap. He explains that the reason "positive thinking" doesn't work for most people is because it only addresses the 1% of our thinking that is conscious, leaving the subconscious mind (which is many times more powerful than the conscious mind) untouched. For this reason, he says that if people really want to change their reality, they must find and consistently practice a technique for reprogramming the subconscious that resonates for them. EFT is one such technique. Other examples include neuro-linguistic programming (NLP), hypnotherapy, and various forms of meditation.

I know of no more effective technique than EFT for getting your subconscious on board with creating a life you really want. If up to 99% of our thinking is unconscious, then obviously any practice that purports to change your point of attraction by "changing your thoughts" must address the subconscious roots of those thoughts. EFT is perhaps the most accessible, and most effective, way to do that. It provides an elegant way to link conscious effort (the Setup and affirmations) with subconscious re-programming (the tapping). Many people (myself included) believe that this is what makes it so effective.

In the coming sections, we're going to explore the three aspects that determine your ability to create an abundant life: *attracting, receiving,* and *having* money. Breaking it down in this way can help you uncover specific events or emotions that form subconscious "bricks" that stand between you and the wealth you want and need. You'll see that there are multiple ways to phrase the Setup to address each specific problem, so it's up to you to determine which resonates the most for you.

Now let's get you started on the road to financial freedom with EFT.

Step 1: Removing Blocks to Attracting Money

In this section, we'll explore how to remove some common subconscious blocks that are specific to *attracting* wealth and abundance. This aspect corresponds to the act of *asking* – we can't receive (much less have) what we don't ask for.

When you imagine asking for more money in your life, what images, memories, or emotions come to mind? As children, many of us experienced asking for things that we wanted very badly and having our parents say "no." If this happens consistently, and especially if our asking prompts a negative emotional response in our parents, we may begin to unconsciously take on the belief that we will never receive the things we want if we ask for them. Then we project these beliefs onto the universe, until we begin to believe that there's no point asking, since the request will only be denied. We would rather deprive ourselves than live with disappointment, so we just stop asking.

Because EFT's effectiveness increases with emotional intensity, it's often best to begin with a specific childhood memory along the lines of the example in the above paragraph. Below are some sample Setup statements:

Setup 1: "Even though my father yelled at me when I asked for a horse because it was too expensive, I deeply love and accept myself."

Setup 2: "Even though my brother made fun of me when I wrote a letter to Santa asking for a million dollars, I deeply love and accept myself."

Setup 3: "Even though most people I asked said no when I tried to sell them Girl Scout cookies in 3rd grade, I deeply love and accept myself."

You can also identify specific emotions that are related to beliefs that may be rooted in these experiences. For example:

Alternate Setup 1: "Even though I have this fear that people/God will be angry with me if I ask for money..."

Alternate Setup 2: "Even though I have this fear that I'll look stupid if I ask for abundance..."

Alternate Setup 3: "Even though I have this fear that the universe won't give me the wealth I ask for..."

You can also work directly on the beliefs that may be causing psychological reversal:

"Even though I have this belief that it's shameful to ask for money...." or
"Even though I have this belief that I'm not worthy to ask for money...."

As you can see the possibilities are endless...you just need to find the Setup that works best for you.

Step 2: Removing Blocks to Receiving Money

Now that you've addressed some of the unconscious "bricks" that are keeping you from asking for the money you want and need, we can begin to remove those that kick in when it's time to receive.

If someone pays you a compliment, do you really take it in, or do you say things like "don't mention it," or "oh, it was nothing." Many of us say such things out of habit, but words are powerful, and when we respond in this way, at some level we are not really letting ourselves receive the love that others offer us. Imagine really letting it in when someone expresses their appreciation for you. What inner reactions do you notice? If you find you have internal resistance to this idea, then you may have discovered some aspects that are preventing you from receiving more money from the Universe. If we want to have more wealth, we have to prime our energy system to let it in, and EFT is an excellent tool for doing that.

So without further ado, here are some sample Setups to amp up your ability to receive the wealth you're now attracting:

Setup 1: "Even though my mother wouldn't let me take the reward that woman offered me when I found and returned her wallet, I deeply love and accept myself."

Setup 2: "Even though that beautiful ring that my high school boyfriend gave me turned out to be stolen, I deeply love and accept myself."

Setup 3: "Even though my father was angry when I took that scholarship instead of 'pulling myself up by my bootstraps,' I deeply love and accept myself."

As in the previous section, you can also identify the specific emotions that may be at the root of these experiences. For example:

Alternate Setup 1: "Even though I have this fear that it's not proper/acceptable/I'm not allowed to receive money, I deeply love and accept myself."

Alternate Setup 2: "Even though I have this fear that receiving money and wealth is unethical, I deeply love and accept myself."

Alternate Setup 3: "Even though I have this fear that people will reject me if I receive wealth without 'earning' it, I deeply love and accept myself."

You can also work directly on the beliefs that may be causing psychological reversal:

"Even though I have this belief that I'm not allowed to receive money...."
"Even though I have this belief that receiving money is unethical...."
"Even though I have this belief that I can't receive money without 'earning' it...."

And so on.

Step 3: Removing Blocks to Having Money

Now that we've addressed subconscious blocks to attracting and receiving money, it's time to take on the final energetic "bricks" that prevent you from *having* the money you want and deserve. This is the moment we've all been waiting for!

If you imagine winning the lottery and suddenly having a hundred million dollars, what inner reactions do you notice? Would you be able to keep that money for yourself, or would you feel compelled to give most of it away to family, friends, or organizations? Can you easily imagine having that much money just sitting in your bank account without mentally creating some reason for it to go away again? More than we realize, many of us hold limiting subconscious beliefs about ourselves and the world that make it impossible for us to *have* money, even if we succeed in asking for and receiving it. Have you ever gotten a financial windfall, only to watch it get eaten up immediately by an equally unexpected expense? When such things happen (and especially if they happen repeatedly), it indicates a strong psychological reversal against having money, usually in the realms of deservedness or safety. These limiting beliefs can run very deep, but EFT provides us with a way to address them effectively, one aspect at a time.

Here are some sample Setups that address the *having* aspect of creating abundance:

Setup 1: "Even though I had that accident right after I received the inheritance from my grandmother, I deeply love and accept myself."

Setup 2: "Even though my father always said that money was the root of all evil, I deeply love and accept myself."

Setup 3: "Even though my parents believed that being wealthy was a sin, I deeply love and accept myself."

Alternate Setup 1: "Even though I have this fear that it's not safe to have money, I deeply love and accept myself."

Alternate Setup 2: "Even though I have this fear that it's not ethical to have money, I deeply love and accept myself."

Alternate Setup 3: "Even though I have this fear that I won't go to heaven if I have money, I deeply love and accept myself."

You can also work directly on the beliefs that may be causing psychological reversal:

"Even though I have this belief that having money is dangerous…."

"Even though I have this belief that 'it's easier for a camel to pass through the eye of a needle than for a rich man to get into heaven….'"

In the next section, I'll offer some final tips for getting the most out of EFT.

Tips for Avoiding Common Pitfalls

Now that you have everything you need to get started using EFT for wealth and abundance, I'll devote one final section to showing you how to avoid common pitfalls that many beginners struggle with. The following should take some frustration out of your initial foray into tapping for wealth, abundance, or anything else.

Pitfall 1: Choosing an issue that is too general or "global."

In *The EFT Manual*, Gary Craig describes this as the most common mistake made by newcomers. He points out that people usually make the most progress with EFT by focusing on specific events or aspects. What's more, addressing these seems to release other aspects of the problem as well. He puts it this way in the *Manual*:

"Perhaps the biggest mistake made by newcomers is that they try to use EFT on issues that are too global. They may make good headway with persistence but they are less likely to notice the results right away. As a result, they may quit too soon. Break the problems down into specific events and you will notice results on those specific events right away. Doing this also addresses the true cause and is usually more efficient."

Some examples of statements that are too global or general to be used in a Setup for tapping include the following:

1. "Even though I have this weight issue…"
2. "Even though I never feel like I have enough money…"
3. "Even though I have low self-worth…"

Each of the issues above contains several emotional aspects, and is more like a "program," going back to our computer analogy from earlier. The contributing aspects, or files, need to be addressed and cleared individually in order for the tapping to work. Below, I outline how this might be done for each example:

1. The problem of 'weight issue' may be mainly composed of fear and shame aspects. It can therefore be broken down into statements like, "I have this shame because of how my body looks" or, "I have

this fear that carrying all this extra weight will eventually kill me."

2. The program of 'never enough money' may be mainly composed of fear and/or anxiety files. It can therefore be broken down into statements like, "I have this fear that I'll lose everything and end up on the street," or, "I have this fear that whenever I do get money it'll be taken away again."

3. 'Low self-worth' may be mainly composed of shame, fear, and judgment. For example, "I have this fear that if people really knew me, they would reject me," or, "I have this fear that I don't deserve to have what I want."

Gary Craig uses the metaphor of a forest in which each aspect of an issue is a diseased tree. In most cases, he says that clearing just a few specific trees (or "aspects" in our case seems to trigger the subconscious to automatically release all remaining related aspects. He gives a real example of someone who experienced countless distinct episodes of childhood abuse, but found complete relief from the emotional turmoil it caused them after tapping on only a handful of specific memories. He refers to this phenomenon as the Generalization Effect in the manual.

Pitfall 2: Focusing too much on the script/making the technique more complicated than it needs to be.

I addressed this earlier in the book, but it bears repeating: *the right Setup can be found in whatever your self-talk is right now.* Don't let your mind sabotage your healing by distracting you from the tapping itself, which is what really helps. The important thing is to do the tapping consistently, on whatever happens to be up for you right now. Because of the generalization effect, this will give you the most bang for your buck in your EFT practice.

Pitfall 3: Not tapping thoroughly enough.

This refers to three areas of your EFT practice:

- Not addressing all aspects of an issue.
- Not getting the discomfort level down to zero.
- Focusing too much on the physical mechanics of tapping, rather than on maintaining the emotional intensity that keeps your meridians blocked so they can respond to the tapping.

Pitfall 4: Not using the reminder phrase / "skimming the negative"

Unfortunately, the "positive thinking" zealots of the self-help movement have trained many of us to avoid acknowledging the negativity that we all carry around, convincing us that thinking even briefly of things we don't want will make them manifest in our reality. What they don't realize is that negativity **must** be acknowledged before it can be released. If fact negativity is, a big red flag saying, "Hey, you've got a big bad program over here that you probably want to get rid of, please tap on me so I can go away!" This is why using the "reminder phrase" while tapping is so crucial to the effectiveness of EFT. Ted Robinson of the Center for Inner Healing puts it this way:

The biggest mistake beginning tappers make is not using negative wording while they tap. This usually stops them from fully feeling the negative feeling or self-limiting belief, and they don't fully unblock their meridians. That means they don't get the best results because there was no blockage in place to tap away with EFT. The best thing to do is fully feel the emotional pain, worry, and stress, and then tell your story about the issue while you tap all the points.

If you really want to become free, you must be willing to sit in the dark for few moments, really feel those nasty emotions, and "call up the negative files" that the tapping is meant to help you clear. After that, you can spend as much time as you want repeating your affirmations, and they will actually stand a chance of doing you some good.

Pitfall 5: Not using the Personal Peace Procedure.

This is the practice I mentioned before, where you create a comprehensive list of past events that carry a negative charge for you and tap on one of them every day. This is an invaluable way to keep up the momentum you generate through EFT, even when you don't have something specific that you feel you need to work on.

Pitfall 6: Taking on more than you can handle alone.

While EFT is a very simple and effective technique, very often the issues we wish to address with it are complex. One reason that working on your issues alone can be frustrating is that it's nearly impossible to see our own "stuff" clearly, so it can take us much longer to get to the root of the problem on our own, if we even get there at all. Any program for personal growth and healing can be made much more effective by working with a trained facilitator, and EFT is no exception. That's why, if you really want results, it is worth seeking the support of a certified EFT practitioner to help you hone in on what it is you *really* need to tap on.

The bottom line is, people often start tapping on issues that are way over their heads, and are often tapping on the wrong thing. EFT works, but only if we use it correctly. Since most of us are not used to dissecting our own issues, it helps to have the support of someone who can guide our initial efforts to shed light on the dark matter of our subconscious minds.

Remember, you can find a comprehensive directory of certified EFT clinicians at http://www.eftuniverse.com/

Conclusion

Throughout this book, it has been my intention to lay out a clear path to creating greater wealth and abundance in your life with EFT. I have tried to strike an ideal balance between keeping it simple (because it really *is* simple), and showing you how to avoid the most common roadblocks that beginners run into. I hope that you have arrived here feeling ready to take your first steps towards improving your life on all levels with EFT.

As you put what you learned in this book into practice, remember that there are three aspects to address when you're tapping to create a more abundant life: *asking for, receiving,* and *having* wealth. I've found that when I break the issue down in this way, it becomes easier to uncover the specific aspects that can help me utilize the generalization effect for maximum results. I feel confident that the same will be true for you.

I recommend reviewing the section on avoiding common pitfalls each time you prepare for a tapping session when you're first starting out. This will help keep your focus where it needs to be in order to generate optimal results. Above all, I urge you to let go of trying to control the technique with your mind, because you'll make the most progress when you let go and trust the process of healing your subconscious with EFT. The more you trust it, the easier it will be for the tapping to do its work.

It's been my privilege to guide you at this stage in your journey, and I congratulate you on taking the next step towards creating the abundant life you want and deserve. With perseverance and consistency, I feel confident that you will soon notice a change in your inner point of attraction around asking for, receiving and having money, and once you've made that inner transformation, your external reality must change to reflect it.

Wishing you peace, joy, and fulfillment on your journey to a bigger and brighter life.

Namaste,

Lisa Townsend

Check out these other books by Lisa Townsend!!

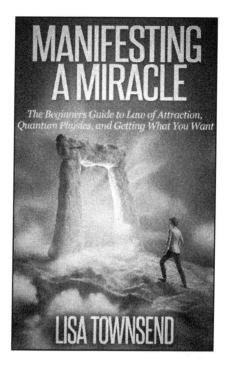

http://www.amazon.com/dp/B00IXCUGWE

http://www.amazon.com/dp/B00IX71JQQ

http://www.amazon.com/dp/B00K1N9Q56